HABITS
— OF —
HOLY MEN

DON H. STAHELI

LLOYD D. NEWELL

DESERET
BOOK

Salt Lake City, Utah

Book design © 2018 Deseret Book Company
Cover design by Shauna Gibby

© 2018 Lloyd D. Newell and Don H. Staheli

All rights reserved. No part of this book may be reproduced in any form or by any means without permission in writing from the publisher, Deseret Book Company at permissions@deseretbook.com or PO Box 30178, Salt Lake City, Utah 84130. This work is not an official publication of The Church of Jesus Christ of Latter-day Saints. The views expressed herein are the responsibility of the authors and do not necessarily represent the position of the Church or of Deseret Book Company.

DESERET BOOK is a registered trademark of Deseret Book Company.

Visit us at DeseretBook.com

Library of Congress Cataloging-in-Publication Data
Names: Staheli, Don H. | Newell, Lloyd D.
Title: Habits of holy men / Don H. Staheli, Lloyd D. Newell.
Description: Salt Lake City, Utah : Deseret Book, [2018] | Includes bibliographical references and index.
Identifiers: LCCN 2018001531 | ISBN 9781629724478 (hardbound : alk. paper)
Subjects: LCSH: Mormons—Religious life. | Mormons—Conduct of life. | Spiritual life—The Church of Jesus Christ of Latter-day Saints. | Holiness—The Church of Jesus Christ of Latter-day Saints. | Christian life—Mormon authors.
Classification: LCC BX8656 .S72 2018 | DDC 248.8/42—dc23
LC record available at https://lccn.loc.gov/2018001531

Printed in the United States of America
Edwards Brothers Malloy, Ann Arbor, MI

10 9 8 7 6 5 4 3 2 1

CONTENTS

Preface v

1. Practice Holiness 1

2. Put Off the Natural Man 7

3. Be Submissive 15

4. Be Meek. 25

5. Be Humble 35

6. Be Patient. 47

7. Be Full of Love. 59

8. Be as a Child 72

9. Conclusion 80

Notes 85

PREFACE

This attempt to write a book on the habits of holiness presupposes some personal understanding of holiness and of the process of achieving this sacred condition. We do not, however, pretend to be "holier than thou" or to know all the answers. Like you, we are striving for a greater measure of holiness in our own lives; we, too, are trying to become holier, better men. Much of what we have learned about the process comes from what we have observed in others, particularly our wonderful wives. We are all, as children of a loving Heavenly Father, endowed with the capacity to refine our lives and become more like our Divine Parents. Our sincere hope is that we may learn together and, through trial and error, mistakes and repentance, make progress along the straight and narrow path that will lead us back into the presence of God. The purpose of this brief tome is to give a little insight that will tighten your grip on the iron rod and bring you greater hope and joy. The writing of it has certainly done so for us.

We greatly appreciate the assistance we have received from Liz Wagner, Tracy Keck, and the Deseret Book team—as well as Ted Barnes for his editorial expertise. We are most grateful for the love, kindness, and holy examples of our wives, Cyndy and Karmel.

Chapter One

PRACTICE HOLINESS

When you think of a holy man, what comes to mind? You may picture a monk in a scratchy, brown robe, living an ascetic life of contemplation and seclusion. Or you may imagine a religious zealot practicing his beliefs to the extreme, living a life of severity and exclusion. These examples probably do not represent how you would want to practice your faith. Yet, like most Latter-day Saint men, you do want to live a life of devotion to the Savior, a life that resembles His to some small degree—a life of holiness that will be acceptable to Him and will lead you and your family back into the presence of God.

To live this kind of holy life, it is essential to understand the principles of the gospel of Jesus Christ, as well as some aspects of behavior—or habits of holiness—that will help you achieve it. Faith and wisdom dictate that if you do the right thing, the right result will follow. By practicing the habits of holiness, you will be doing the right thing, and—in part in this life and in a fullness in the next—you will become holy.

BUT WHAT IS HOLINESS?

For the purposes of this book, think of holiness simply as harmony with God. The holy man has learned to harmonize his will with the will of Heavenly Father. "Jesus works under the direction of the Father and is in complete harmony with Him."[1] To the degree that it is humanly possible, the holy man will strive to harmonize his life with God, just as Jesus did.

Holiness, your personal harmony with Heavenly Father, is more than an attitude or a religious philosophy. Holiness is a devoted way of life that reflects obedience to the commandments of God and a sincere desire to subject your will to His. A holy man's efforts are not perfect, but he keeps striving, trusts in God, and does his best to live habits of holiness. Remember, holiness in the here and now does not mean perfection (see Matthew 5:48, footnote *b*). It means your heart and mind are right with God and you are doing your best to be true.

A HOLY HEART

Unlike worldly success, which is often defined by external achievements and material accumulation, holiness is measured by looking at the heart. The prophet Samuel's search for a new king of Israel is a good example of this truth. The Lord directed Samuel to the house of Jesse, where the new king was to be found and anointed. When Samuel saw Jesse's son Eliab, he was impressed by Eliab's size and appearance. Eliab looked like a king! Surely this was the man. But the Lord corrected Samuel right away, saying, "Look not on his countenance, or on the height of his stature; . . . for the Lord seeth not as man seeth; for man looketh on the outward appearance, but the Lord looketh on the heart" (1 Samuel 16:7). Eventually Samuel met Jesse's youngest son, David, likely just a teenager. Though David's appearance was youthful and he was not as charismatic as his brother, David's heart was right, and he was anointed king.

Deep down, men want to be judged by their heart, not by their outward appearance, but we often have trouble letting people see that side of us or even accessing it ourselves. Our feelings may not be all that open to review, but that doesn't mean they don't exist. Men can be tender and emotional, but we are often unlikely to show it. With a little introspection, men can feel the need for holiness and long for the closeness to God that it implies.

SWEET IS THE WORK

Achieving holiness does take work—hard, consistent, time-consuming, sometimes heartbreaking, often exhilarating work. As A. W. Tozer wrote in his book *The Pursuit of God*: "Come near to the holy men and women of the past and you will soon feel the heat of their desire after God. They mourned for Him, they prayed and wrestled and sought Him day and night, in season and out, and when they had found Him the finding was all the sweeter for the long seeking."[2]

We speak often of enduring to the end. Endurance leading to holiness is hard work. It requires stamina and a deep willingness to undergo stress without giving in to the desire to quit. Jesus gave this counsel to the Nephites: "Look unto me, and endure to the end, and ye shall live; for unto him that endureth to the end will I give eternal life" (3 Nephi 15:9). Thankfully, the Lord will not require of us more than we are able to give. Just as God will not suffer that we are tempted above that which we are able to bear (see 1 Corinthians 10:13), He will not ask us to endure more than He knows we can manage, which may be far more than we believe we can. Our loving Father knows our limits. We are each on a personal and individualized journey to the summit of our potential. Like the climb up a mountain, the pathway to holiness is steep and can be intimidating, but the views from holy heights are stunning and worth every challenging step.

HOLY COVENANTS AND PRIESTHOOD

One of the ways we practice holiness is by making covenants with God and keeping the promises we make to Him. There is a difference between a covenant and a promise. A promise can be unilateral: "I promise you." It is a sign of submission that does not depend on reciprocation from another party. A covenant is mutual; we make it *with* someone. It requires another party with whom we make a binding agreement. While promises can stand alone and remain in force regardless of the actions of another, covenants bind us to one another, and their efficacy is dependent on the actions of both parties.

There is profound meaning in the word *keep*. In addition to the common uses of the word, as in "keep a secret" or "keep the Sabbath day holy," there is the connotation that comes with the phrase "keep from harm." In the beautiful Loire Valley in France are magnificent castles, or *chateaux*. Some of them are surrounded by high walls with an open area in the center. This area is called the *keep*. The keep is the portion of the castle where the inhabitants can feel safest from outside dangers. All the protective resources available are put in place to keep them from harm. So too, when we *keep* the commandments and *keep* our covenants, all the spiritual protection of heaven is brought to bear in our behalf. And truly, the home, our personal "castle," is the first line of defense.[3] The greatest protection is found in a covenant-keeping home presided over by a worthy patriarch who honors his priesthood.

A covenant that is unique to men is the oath and covenant of the priesthood (see D&C 84:33–41). The Lord has chosen to give the keys of the priesthood to men. With that incredible gift comes the great responsibility to magnify it—to enlarge or amplify the influence of the priesthood. This can be done only in holiness.

PRACTICE MAKES PERFECT

In January 1831, when the fledgling restored Church of Jesus Christ was less than a year old, the Lord commanded the Saints to love one another and to "practice virtue and holiness before me" (D&C 38:24). Just weeks later, in March 1831, the people of the Church were "commanded in all things to ask of God, who giveth liberally; and that which the Spirit testifies unto you even so I would that ye should do in all holiness of heart," and the Lord repeated the imperative that they "must practice virtue and holiness before me continually" (D&C 46:7, 33). The use of the word *practice* implies that holiness is a spiritual skill that can be practiced and must be cultivated. As with other skills, the more we practice, the more adept we become.

None of us really expects to be perfect in this life, yet we must strive every day to become more whole, more complete, and closer to perfection. A fully holy state is unlikely to be achieved during our mortal existence. But practice we must, and, as Ralph Waldo Emerson said, "That which we persist in doing becomes easier to do, not that the nature of the thing has changed but that our power to do has increased."

Chapter Two

PUT OFF THE NATURAL MAN

Every six months, the semiannual general conference of The Church of Jesus Christ of Latter-day Saints convenes. Some 20,000 people gather in the Conference Center in Salt Lake City to hear the words of the chosen servants of the Lord. Millions more join the congregation via television, satellite, the internet, and other media sources.

General conference is sometimes compared to a similar gathering that took place in Book of Mormon times. About 124 years before the coming of Christ, Benjamin, king of the Nephites, was nearing the end of his life. Before he died, he asked his son Mosiah to send out a proclamation that all the people should gather at the temple so he could announce the appointment of his son as king and address his people one last time.

The people gathered as families, pitching their tents with the doors facing the temple. The crowd was so large that King Benjamin had a tower built upon which he could stand to deliver his discourse. In addition, his words were written and distributed to all who could not hear him (see Mosiah 1:10–2:8). The media of that day was simple yet effective.

DISCOVERING HABITS OF HOLINESS

King Benjamin's discourse is full of inspiring counsel that, if followed, will lead to a life of holiness. One particular passage stands out as a concise, almost step-by-step approach to becoming holy. It is found in Mosiah chapter 3, verse 19. It reads: "For the natural man is an enemy to God, and has been from the fall of Adam, and will be, forever and ever, unless he yields to the enticings of the Holy Spirit, and putteth off the natural man and becometh a saint through the atonement of Christ the Lord, and becometh *as a child, submissive, meek, humble, patient, full of love,* willing to submit to all things which the Lord seeth fit to inflict upon him, even as a child doth submit to his father" (emphasis added).

In this verse, we discover some key habits of holiness:

Be submissive (stated twice, like bookends to the process): willingly yielding to the will of Heavenly Father and Jesus Christ.

Be meek: not power hungry; generously using one's talents and abilities to bless others.

Be humble: teachable, connected to God, and completely devoid of self-interest.

Be patient: supportive and helpful as others progress.

Be full of love: striving for Christlike compassion.

Be as a child: clean, innocent, and trusting.

As we nurture any one of these habits, we nurture them all. To work on one of them is to work on each of them.

THE NATURAL MAN IN EACH OF US

Because of the Fall, we all have something of the natural man in us. Robert L. Millet taught: "We all have inherited Adam and Eve's fallen nature, which includes the ability and the propensity to sin. . . . Conception, which clothes us in the flesh, is the mechanism of transmission, the means by which Adam and Eve's fallen nature (both physical and spiritual death) is transferred from generation to generation. The propensity for and susceptibility to sin are implanted in our nature at conception, just as death is."[4]

By our very nature, we will all commit sins of varying degrees of seriousness. As part of His plan of eternal happiness, the Father sent His Only Begotten Son to atone for our sins and pave the way for our forgiveness. We have been given time and instruction that allow us to repent and do better (see Alma 12:22–24). Rather than dwelling on a painful past or fearing for the future, our best choice is to accept our current circumstances, learn from and see the good in them, move forward to improve ourselves, and become what our Father knows we can be.

Sister Carol F. McConkie spoke of this process when she said: "Our hope for holiness is centered in Christ, in His mercy and His grace. With faith in Jesus Christ and His Atonement, we may become clean, without spot, when we deny ourselves of ungodliness and sincerely repent. We are baptized by water for the remission of sins. Our souls are sanctified when we receive the Holy Ghost with open hearts. Weekly, we partake of the ordinance of the sacrament. In a spirit of repentance, with sincere desires for righteousness, we covenant that we are willing to take upon us the name of Christ, remember Him, and keep His commandments so that we may always have His Spirit to be with us. Over time, as we continually strive to become one with the Father, the Son, and the Holy Ghost, we become partakers of Their divine nature."[5] We will become holy.

THE STORY OF NAAMAN

One scriptural account that illustrates the habits of holiness is the intriguing story of Elisha and Naaman in the Old Testament (see 2 Kings 5).

About 800 B.C., Naaman was the captain of the armies of Syria. He was "a mighty man in valour" and led military campaigns for the king of Syria, "but he was a leper" (2 Kings 5:1). At that time, leprosy was usually a death sentence, as the leper was literally eaten alive by aggressive bacteria. Because the disease was spread by contact, lepers were sent away to live in their misery with other victims of the dreaded plague.

What a shock it must have been for Naaman, a man of means and power, to be diagnosed with a problem over which he had absolutely no control. He must have been desperate for any help he could find. Little did he know that he would discover the solution to his problem in the advice of a servant girl.

In those days, raiding companies of soldiers made excursions into neighboring countries to capture people and bring them back as slaves. Naaman had such a person, a "little maid" (verse 2) of the land of Israel, who worked in his household as a servant for his wife. When she heard of her master's plight, she boldly suggested that there was a man in Samaria—a prophet—who could heal him.

As anyone with a serious disease would agree, any potential cure is worth pursuing. You never know what might work! So Naaman sought the diplomatic intervention of his king, who sent a letter and a great deal of money to the king of Israel, who ruled Samaria. The Syrian king's message said, in effect, "Here is Naaman. Cure him!"

Of course, the king of Israel was terrified by this demand. He was no healer. He thought the king of Syria was just trying to set him up—"Heal Naaman, or the next visit will be from my armies!"

Luckily, as the biblical account reveals, the man who actually could help heard about the problem. His name was

Elisha. A man of God, Elisha was known for his remarkable accomplishments. "Let [Naaman] come now to me," he said, with great confidence that he could help Naaman overcome his trouble (verse 8). Before long, Naaman, with his horses and chariot, was at Elisha's doorstep.

Considering himself a man to be reckoned with, Naaman expected Elisha to come out of the house, and with prophetic declaration, pronounce him clean. But no. Elisha sent only a messenger, someone far beneath Naaman's social station. Worse still, the messenger simply told Naaman to go and bathe seven times in the local river, and he would be clean.

"Naaman was wroth, and went away, and said, Behold, I thought, He will surely come out to me, and stand, and call on the name of the Lord his God, and strike his hand over the place, and recover the leper. Are not Abana and Pharpar, rivers of Damascus, better than all the waters of Israel? may I not wash in them, and be clean? So he turned and went away in a rage" (verses 11–12).

Soon, cooler heads prevailed, and one of Naaman's servants approached him carefully. The servant brought up the obvious fact that Naaman had been ready to do some difficult and spectacular deed to be relieved of his affliction. Why not something easy, like washing in a river?

Naaman must have realized there was nothing to be gained from his childish response, so he headed for the nearby river. He dipped himself seven times in the river Jordan, "and his flesh came again like unto the flesh of a little child, and he was clean" (verse 14).

It had worked! He was no longer a leper. Recovering from leprosy was unheard of, but it had happened to Naaman. Just imagine how he must have felt. His flesh had been terribly infected, and a sentence of grotesque deformity and slow death had been pronounced, but his skin was now as smooth and clear as a baby's.

Based on this experience, and surely on the workings of the Spirit, Naaman's faith in Jehovah was set. "Behold," he said to Elisha, "now I know that there is no God in all the earth, but in Israel" (verse 15). Naaman tried to pay Elisha for his service, but this offer was summarily refused. Elisha had no thought of personal gain.

THE HABITS OF HOLINESS EXEMPLIFIED

By analyzing this unique and interesting story, we can see the habits of holiness exemplified:

Be submissive: Though Naaman struggled at first when Elisha instructed him to do something different from what he had anticipated, he was ultimately submissive to the prophet's direction.

Be meek: Naaman's servants could see that he needed their encouragement. They approached him meekly, willing to take the risk of crossing the line between servant and master.

Be humble: Naaman knew he needed help. After

overcoming his ego, he was willing to be taught and guided in seeking a cure.

Be patient: Naaman was patient with his servants as they tried to help him. He was also patient with the prescribed treatment of his disease—he dipped himself all seven times.

Be full of love: There is a lot of love and compassion demonstrated in this story—the love of the servants for Naaman, the love of Elisha for the Syrian who came to his door, the compassion of the Lord toward a seeker, and the love of the Lord that Naaman felt after his cure.

Be as a child: The childlike faith of the handmaiden of Naaman's wife is the foundation for the whole episode.

Try to notice these habits in your own life and the lives of those around you, and watch for the joy and power they bring. The habits of holiness are observable in every effort to repent, to be obedient, and to do the will of God. As you study the scriptures and the remaining chapters of this book, you will learn more and more about their application in your efforts to live a life of holiness.

Chapter Three

BE SUBMISSIVE

In May 1945, a trembling, eighteen-year-old soldier named Neal Maxwell knelt in a muddy foxhole in Okinawa, Japan. He was in the midst of one of the fiercest battles of World War II, and an artillery shell had just landed five feet away from him. In a panic, Neal "spoke the deepest prayer he had ever uttered, pleading for protection and dedicating the rest of his life to the Lord's service."[6]

The next day, several shells were launched at Neal's location, but not one of them exploded. The Lord honored Neal's prayer, and Neal honored his commitment, which proved to be much more than a "foxhole promise." Over the subsequent decades, submission to God—turning one's life over to Him and His will—became a notable theme not only of Elder Neal A. Maxwell's many sermons and writings as an Apostle[7] but also of his life. Elder Maxwell spent his apostolic ministry teaching us why and how we can become more submissive, more consecrated to the Lord.

Perhaps the most poignant example came shortly after Elder Maxwell was diagnosed with leukemia in October 1996. The outlook was not good—survival rates for people his age were discouragingly low, and doctors predicted that he would live only a few more months. Decades of training his heart to submit to God's will had now made him surprisingly comfortable accepting his fate. He didn't feel he deserved any kind of special miracle, so he wasn't inclined to request one.

But his wife, Colleen, had a different opinion. Wasn't it the Savior Himself, she reminded her husband, who pleaded in the Garden of Gethsemane, "If it be possible, let this cup pass from me" before eventually saying, "Nevertheless not as I will, but as thou wilt" (Matthew 26:39)? Perhaps it was possible to plead for a miracle while also being perfectly submissive to God's will.[8]

As it turned out, it was God's will for Elder Maxwell's life to be extended. A miracle did occur, and he lived and served another eight years. At Elder Maxwell's funeral, President Gordon B. Hinckley commented that his friend had "accomplished more in these last eight years than most men do in a lifetime. . . . I think we shall not see one like him again."[9]

In some ways, it probably would have been easier to quietly pass away after being diagnosed with such a fatal disease at the age of seventy. Elder Maxwell's final years were filled with painful, exhausting chemotherapy treatments and intensive medical attention. Accepting an extension of his life had implications that were both dreadful and miraculous. This final test of submissiveness brought a sacred experience that Elder Maxwell compared with that night in the foxhole in Okinawa. The Spirit whispered to his mind, "I have given you leukemia that you might teach my people with authenticity." The words sank deep into his soul, confirming his belief that his suffering, as well as his prolonged life, was part of the Lord's plan for him.[10] After a courageous struggle, Elder Maxwell passed away in July 2004 at the age of seventy-eight.

Even as we reflect with admiration on the life of someone like Neal A. Maxwell, it's clear that we live in a world where submissiveness isn't exactly a prized possession. No, ours is a culture of consuming self-centeredness and self-sufficiency—one that says, "I need only me; I trust only me; I can rely only on me." As men, in particular, we prize rugged individualism and robust self-reliance. We are told, "Be yourself. Do your own thing. Follow your own way." Christ, on the other hand, beckons, "Follow me" (Mark 8:34). To see our nothingness before God and become submissive disciples of Christ is the quest of a lifetime (see Mosiah 4:5, 11).

That's easier said than done. As Elder Maxwell put it: "The descriptive simplicity of [submissiveness] is matched by its developmental difficulty. It is so easy to be halfhearted, but this only produces half the growth, half the blessings, and just half a life, really, with more bud than blossom."[11]

SWALLOWED UP IN THE JOY OF CHRIST

Of course, it would be easy to submit to God's will if we believed His will was to make our life worry-free and as comfortable as possible. Perhaps part of our hesitation to fully submit is our sneaking suspicion that God's will might include some pain and suffering.

Submitting our will to God's, by definition, means doing something we may not want to do. Why would anyone do that? If the purpose of life is to find happiness, doesn't that mean we should avoid anything unpleasant or uncomfortable?

But happiness doesn't seem to work that way, does it? As President Russell M. Nelson taught: "We can feel joy even while having a bad day, a bad week, or even a bad year! . . . We can feel joy regardless of what is happening—or not happening—in our lives."[12]

Yes, we are here to find happiness, but we're also here to learn and grow, to progress along the pathway of discipleship. Joy is part of that journey, but so is adversity—the two are not mutually exclusive.

Trials are unavoidable but are also refining—if we respond to them correctly. Followers of Christ in all dispensations are no strangers to sorrow. They know pain up close and personal, and they are well acquainted with affliction. In fact, you might say that affliction is one of the defining characteristics of God's covenant people—not because it is unique to us but because it plays such a critical role in making us who we are and what we have the potential to become. As the Lord reminded Israel, "I have refined thee, I have chosen thee in the furnace of affliction" (1 Nephi 20:10). The tempered steel of faith is forged in the flames of suffering. Ease and comfort do not call forth the greatness of character or the strength of commitment that is needed today.

However, it is not the affliction itself but our response to it that brings the refining. The crucibles of life simply give us opportunities—opportunities to become better or bitter, refined or rebellious, submissive or stiff-necked. If we choose to submit to God's desires to refine and purify us through our trials and challenges, then His peace can carry us through adversities that would otherwise crush us. This doesn't mean that we try to ignore the heartache or deny the reality of the pain. Rather, we take an authentic look at it, enlarging our perspective by believing that some good can come from life's crucible experiences.

For the submissive man, the afflictions of life are "swallowed up in the joy of Christ" (Alma 31:38). Our afflictions and troubles, our heartache and pain may not disappear, but we see them from the wide-angle perspective of eternity, as "but a small moment" that, if we endure well, will end in our exaltation (D&C 121:7–8). With our steady pursuit of submissiveness, with each increasing measure of righteousness, we will experience one more drop of devotion, one more ounce of peace, one more measure of joy (see Alma 26:11).

SUBMISSIVENESS IS ESSENTIAL TO PRIESTHOOD SERVICE

It may be that one of the reasons God gave His priesthood to His sons was to teach us submissiveness. You can't go very far in priesthood service before you realize that if you try to do it your way instead of the Lord's way, you don't accomplish much. Submissiveness guides the priesthood holder to do his duty and willingly fulfill callings, to look for opportunities to serve and help others, to treat all people with integrity and compassion, and to put first things first as he leads his family in love and righteousness. The more we can do this, the closer our service comes to this stunning description in Joseph Smith's translation of the book of Genesis: "Every one being ordained after this order and calling should have power, by faith, to break mountains, to divide the seas, to dry up waters, to turn them out of their course; to put at defiance the armies of nations, to divide the earth, to break every band, to stand in the presence of God; to do all things *according to his will, according to his command,* subdue principalities and powers; and this *by the will of the Son of God*" (JST—Genesis 14:30–31; emphasis added).

"BUT IF NOT..."

Now, lest we think that to be submissive means to be timid, shy, and easily intimidated, let's look at a story from the Old Testament. It's about three young men who, like Neal A.

Maxwell, epitomize submissiveness to the Lord. They too had made a commitment to Him, but they lived in a place where the Lord was barely acknowledged, let alone worshipped. Their names were Shadrach, Meshach, and Abed-nego, and they were Israelites taken captive into Babylon to serve King Nebuchadnezzar. Because of their goodness and purity, they had begun to gain favor in the eyes of the king, but all that changed when Nebuchadnezzar erected a 90-foot golden image.

Imagine what it might have been like to be present at the dedication ceremony for this imposing monument. There must have been a sense of excitement and awe surrounding the event. It was announced to the gathered crowds that when they heard the music play, everyone was to bow down and worship the king's monument. Anyone refusing would be thrown into a furnace of fire.

Perhaps there were others, including other Israelite captives, who were hesitant to worship the golden idol. But when the music sounded, everyone knelt—everyone except Shadrach, Meshach, and Abed-nego. Their defiance was brought to the king's attention, and he flew into a rage. He demanded that they be brought before him and repeated his threat: "If ye worship not, ye shall be cast the same hour into the midst of a burning fiery furnace; and who is that God that shall deliver you out of my hands?" (Daniel 3:15).

Boldly they responded: "Our God whom we serve is able

to deliver us from the burning fiery furnace. . . . But if not, be it known unto thee, O king, that we will not serve thy gods, nor worship the golden image which thou hast set up" (Daniel 3:17–18).

With these three submissive words, "but if not," Shadrach, Meshach, and Abed-nego vowed they would serve God no matter the cost, no matter the consequences, no matter the risks. They knew He had the power to deliver them—and that would probably be their preference!—but they were willing to submit to His will, whatever it was, rather than betray Him. Even if He allowed them to suffer, nothing would persuade them to do anything that they saw as contrary to His will.

This same lesson appears in the submissiveness of Abraham, who somehow brought himself to bind his beloved son Isaac and raise the knife to offer him as a sacrifice, for no other apparent reason than that the Lord had commanded it (see Genesis 22). And it is poignantly taught and epitomized by the Son of God Himself, who, at the height of His suffering in behalf of all of us, hoped that there might be another way. "Father," He said, "if thou be willing, remove this cup from me: nevertheless not my will, but thine, be done" (Luke 22:42).

Clearly, submissiveness is not cowardly or passive. In most cases, it is the ultimate expression of courage and faith.

POWER, LOVE, AND A SOUND MIND

In 2 Timothy 1:7 the Lord gives us a powerful reminder: "God hath not given us the spirit of fear; but of power, and of love, and of a sound mind." These words suggest not only the antidote for fear but also a fitting description of a man who submits to the Lord's will. Submission brings true **power**; so often it is our own stubborn insistence on doing things our way that prevents God's power from flowing into our lives. Submission is inspired by **love**; the more we love the Lord—and recognize how much He loves us—the easier it is to accept His will for us, to want what He wants. Submission requires a **sound mind**; it is facilitated by a clear understanding of God's eternal plan for us, and it demands a conscious choice and the willful and authentic exercise of moral agency. Like all of the habits of holiness, it is not for the weak or fainthearted.

We conclude this chapter as we began, with Elder Neal A. Maxwell: "The submission of one's will is really the only uniquely personal thing we have to place on God's altar. The many other things we 'give,' brothers and sisters, are actually the things He has already given or loaned to us. However, when you and I finally submit ourselves, by letting our individual wills be swallowed up in God's will, then we are really giving something to Him! It is the only possession which is truly ours to give! Consecration thus constitutes the only unconditional surrender which is also a total victory!"[13]

Submissiveness brings us closer to God and His Son, closer to becoming like Them and developing a heart like Theirs. By keeping our eyes and our heart focused upon the Lord, we will be enabled by the power of the Atonement to surrender our will and submit to His tutoring hand and loving grace through good times and bad, through the ups and downs of our mortal journey. Our motives, our desires, and our attitudes are refined as each day we choose to submissively turn to the Lord, little by little, in small but meaningful ways. In our own life's foxholes, we dedicate ourselves to God, and we find that He has already dedicated Himself to us.

Chapter Four

BE MEEK

One of my clearest childhood memories[14] is of going with my father to inspect a home he had leased to a family. I think I was around nine or ten years old. My parents had purchased the home to bring in a little extra money for their family of nine. The renters had moved out after living there for several years, and Dad and I were going to get the place ready for new renters. My dad was good at home repairs and maintenance, so he spent a lot of time taking care of the property. He sometimes brought me along to help.

I'll never forget what I saw when we walked into the home that day. It was a disaster! I can still see it all these years later: trash everywhere, stained carpets and floors, filthy bathrooms. The walls even had holes and scribblings on them. I grew up in a home of seven children, so I was familiar with untidiness, but

I had never seen anything like this! What made it worse, in my mind, was the fact that my father, out of the goodness of his heart, had let the family live there at a reduced rate.

Dad quietly assessed the mess, made note of what needed to be done, and started to work. My adolescent anger boiled—both at the family and at my dad. "Why don't you go after them?" I demanded in exasperation. "You know where they've moved. Go after them. Make them pay for all this!"

My father was quiet as he walked around the home and listened to my rant. Then calmly he said, "They knew better than this. They had agreed to take care of it and clean it. But maybe something has happened in their family. I'm not going to let them ruin my day."

I was stunned. I was mad. They already *had* ruined his day—not to mention mine. Now we had to spend our own time and money making repairs that weren't our fault. This wasn't fair. I wanted justice. I wanted an eye for an eye, a tooth for a tooth. I wanted to call the police. Or, better yet, to go find these people and trash their new home and show them what it felt like. Something! But my father just calmly set to work.

Now that I've gained a few years and a little more experience and wisdom, now that I've worked at becoming a better man, my father's words ring in my ears with a little more clarity: "I'm not going to let them ruin my day." He wasn't referring to home repairs and cleaning. What would have ruined the day for him was the anger, the indignant, vengeful attitude. I am amazed at his strength of character, his equanimity, his self-control. All these years later, I'm embarrassed at my childish fuming.

My father was a strong man who had a goodness about him that radiated to others. He passed away more than thirty years ago, but my six siblings and I would never think of him as weak or wimpy or afraid. He worked in a steel mill and was somehow able to preserve a gentle spirit in that rough environment. He trusted the Lord and never wavered through all the ups and downs and challenges of life. He knew who he was, and he was not weak in any way. But he *was* meek.

When I think of the virtue of meekness, I think of two people: the Savior Jesus Christ and my father. Truly, I was blessed to be reared in a home with a father who was meek.

MEEK AND LOWLY IN HEART

So what does it mean to be meek? Consider this example from the Savior—one of the sweetest and most powerful moments of His ministry. The setting is the Last Supper, a private gathering of Jesus' closest associates, just hours before He gave His life as a sacrifice to save mankind:

"He riseth from supper, and laid aside his garments; and took a towel, and girded himself. After that he poureth water into a basin, and began to wash the disciples' feet, and to wipe them with the towel wherewith he was girded" (John 13:4–5).

The disciples must have been astounded. Their Lord and Master, the man whom they worshipped as the Son of God, was kneeling before them, performing a service that, in their minds, belonged to lowly servants. Perhaps sensing their amazement, Jesus asked:

"Know ye what I have done to you? Ye call me Master and Lord: and ye say well; for so I am. If I then, your Lord and Master, have washed your feet; ye also ought to wash one another's feet. For I have given you an example, that ye should do as I have done to you" (John 13:12–15).

This simple model speaks volumes about what it means to be meek. Meekness is not fear or cowering. Jesus was meek not because He was intimidated or powerless. Meekness, rather, is great power—used gently, quietly, and humbly in the service of others.

That's so different from the way the world views and uses power; perhaps that is why meekness is such an underappreciated virtue and such a misunderstood principle. As the Master taught His disciples when they were found arguing about position and prominence: "Ye know that the princes of the Gentiles exercise dominion over them, and they that are great exercise authority upon them. But it shall not be so among you: but whosoever will be great among you, let him be your minister; And whosoever will be chief among you, let him be your servant" (Matthew 20:25–27).

The world puts a lot of pressure on men to seek power

BE MEEK

and influence. Most of the world's cultures teach men, from an early age, to evaluate our importance and success by the leadership positions we achieve, and leadership is defined by how many people are under our command. But the kingdom of God is not like the kingdoms of the world in at least one important detail: greatness is not measured by how many people serve us but by how many people we serve. Said another way, greatness is measured by meekness.

Alma the Younger is one who learned this lesson about meekness. During his rebellious days, he was known as "a man of many words" who had a powerful influence over the opinions and actions of others. Unfortunately, he used his skills and influence to lead "many of the people to do after the manner of his iniquities" (Mosiah 27:8).

After his conversion, Alma's heart changed, and so did the spirit of his efforts. He was still a man of many words—a good portion of the words in the Book of Mormon are Alma's—and he still had a powerful influence on others. But now he used this power not to destroy the Church but to "impart much consolation to the church, confirming their faith, and exhorting them with long-suffering and much travail" (verse 33). Instead of popularity, he faced "much tribulation, being greatly persecuted," all for the sake of being an instrument "in the hands of God in bringing many to . . . the knowledge of their Redeemer" (verses 32, 36). In doing so, Alma received greater power from God than he'd ever had on his own, but he always used it according to the will of the Lord, in His service (see, for example, Alma 14:10–11, 14–29). In short, Alma learned how to be meek.

To be meek is to desire righteousness and strive to be more Christlike in our daily walk and talk; to be meek is to counsel with the Lord in all things and always remember Him; to be meek is to be gentle and choose not to take offense or harbor resentment; to be meek is to be forgiving and compassionate; to be meek is to be unpretentious and teachable; but perhaps most importantly, to be meek is to exercise complete self-control.

Meekness changes hearts and homes. Imagine how the virtue of meekness would bless and strengthen a marriage and family, and all our relationships. Consider the spiritual power in a home that is filled with a spirit of meekness, gentleness, and kindness. And think how becoming meeker will give you greater power, confidence, and peace.

BLESSED ARE THE MEEK

Perhaps what gives meekness its particular spiritual power is the influence it has on our hearts. Meekness changes us. Like a plow that loosens thick earth in preparation for planting, meekness prepares us to acquire the other attributes of Christ. Meekness allows us to be teachable. It breaks down the walls of stubbornness and pride that prevent us from progressing. Meekness is not simply a nice quality to have; it is critical to our salvation and exaltation. In fact, Mormon taught that a man "cannot have faith and hope, save he shall be meek, and lowly of heart," and he added that without such attributes, "faith and hope is vain, for none is acceptable before God, save the meek and lowly in heart" (Moroni 7:43–44).

The meek have a desire for righteousness despite the carnal susceptibilities and allurements all around us in this fallen world. At the center of meekness is gratefulness and thanksgiving, seeing blessings and miracles all around us as we acknowledge the source of those blessings. This is why missionaries write home every week about the constant flow of miracles in their work. In their meekness, their eyes and hearts are attuned to the Lord's handiwork.

Meekness comes of knowing that anything we do well is a gift from God. Perhaps therein lies the truth of this statement by the Savior, who was known for both His meekness and His power: "Blessed are the meek: for they shall inherit the earth" (Matthew 5:5).

The meek are willing to believe without demanding further information or explanation from the Lord. Their attitude is like Nephi's: "I know that [God] loveth his children; nevertheless, I do not know the meaning of all things" (1 Nephi 11:17). The meek "trust in the Lord with all [their] heart; and lean not unto [their] own understanding. In all . . . ways [they] acknowledge him, and he shall direct [their] paths" (Proverbs 3:5–6).

As the meek suffer harm and wrongdoing—for life is full of offense, even for those who strive to give none—they choose not to harbor resentment or nurture wounds. The meek choose to move on and move forward. Their love in response to bitterness and anger creates ever-widening circles of kindness and compassion. They have the moral strength to return no evil for evil, to be considerate in the presence of cruelty, and to be gentle in the presence of harshness.

That's the quiet power that comes of meekness. The meek are at peace; they seem to be able to endure harsh words, incivility, and unfairness. The meek do not seek to retaliate—they seek to understand and to heal. Elder Bruce R. McConkie further explained: "The meek are the god fearing and the righteous. They are the ones who willingly conform to the gospel standards, thus submitting their wills to the will of the Lord. They are not the fearful, the spiritless, the timid. Rather, the most forceful, dynamic personality who ever lived—He who drove the money changers from the temple . . . said of Himself, 'I am meek and lowly in heart.'"[15]

LIVE IN THE SPIRIT OF MEEKNESS

Some time ago, one Latter-day Saint striving for holiness shared on a blog his simple "meekness test": "Imagine you are calmly driving to work. Another driver, weaving dangerously through traffic, pulls past on the right and cuts sharply in front of you, causing you to hit your brakes hard enough that the

BE MEEK

person behind you just misses your bumper. How do you react? If your first thoughts include concern for the offender as well as for those affected by the dangerous driving, you are well on your way to the strength and love that meekness requires. 'Father forgive that driver and help him calm down and drive safely.' Choosing to look past offense to love requires meekness. We are often faced with simple tests like this. I fear I fail more than I pass. How long must meekness seek root in my life before it takes a firm hold? . . . If we understand the need for meekness and its requirements, maybe, just maybe, those we deem offenders today will one day become precious to us despite continued mistakes. Perhaps we will view obedience as an opportunity instead of a requirement and self-control as one of the godliest of attributes to seek after. We will see true strength in meekness."[16] Truly, there is strength, peace, and abiding joy in meekness.

During the last moments of His mortal life, the Savior faced a seemingly endless series of injustices. His closest friends failed to watch with Him, betrayed Him, and denied even knowing Him. He was unjustly accused of ridiculous crimes. He was mocked, abused, brutally scourged, and condemned to die. He suffered a torturous death, with the laughter and ridicule of His tormentors ringing in His ears: "He saved others; himself he cannot save" (Mark 15:31).

Well, that observation was partly true. He did save others. But Himself He *could* have saved. He had legions of angels at

His command, and could have, at any time, called upon them to deliver Him from the hands of His enemies (see Matthew 26:53). It must have crossed the minds of at least some of the observers at Golgotha, "Why *isn't* He saving Himself?" They had, many of them, witnessed His miracles on behalf of others. They had seen that there was no disease or ailment—blindness, palsy, leprosy, even death itself—that He could not subdue. So why would He suddenly submit to this suffering?

The answer lies at the heart of meekness. By choosing not to employ His great power to save Himself, using it instead to bear ever-increasing levels of humiliation and suffering in our behalf, the Savior showed us what true meekness—and true power—is. So instead of saving Himself, His thoughts turned to the welfare of those around Him, including those who were in the process of killing Him, and from the bottom of His meek and forgiving heart, He said: "Father, forgive them; for they know not what they do" (Luke 23:34). This is *how* He saved others: by *not* saving Himself. And this act of meekness we call the Atonement of Jesus Christ is also how He empowers us to put off the natural man and become like Him: "submissive, meek, humble, patient, full of love, willing to submit to all things which the Lord seeth fit to inflict upon him, even as [the Perfect Son] doth submit to [the Father]" (Mosiah 3:19).

Chapter Five

BE HUMBLE

Is it possible for a man to be both exceptionally talented and humble? Can he accomplish great things, achieve success and recognition, without becoming self-absorbed? History has given us reason to doubt. It seems that when men are charged with a special task and, through their own diligent work and even a little luck, come out victorious, almost inevitably they fall into the arrogance trap. Even if the accomplishment is noble and moral, it comes with the risk of pride. Praise and adulation are intoxicating drinks.

And yet, every once in a while, we come across men who are at once great and humble. Somehow, they are able to lift others without lifting themselves.

John the Baptist is unique among prophets. He had a starring role in three gospel dispensations: he was the dominant figure in the closing of the Mosaic dispensation; as the forerunner for the Messiah, he helped open the dispensation of the meridian of time; and as a resurrected messenger, he also played a key part in the dispensation of the fullness of times by restoring the Aaronic Priesthood.

His preaching in the wilderness of Judea attracted the attention of common Jews, Pharisees, and even Roman soldiers. The chief priests and elders, who openly criticized Jesus, were afraid to publicly question John's authority, "for all hold John as a prophet" (Matthew 21:26). The Savior Himself declared, "Among those that are born of women there is not a greater prophet than John the Baptist" (Luke 7:28). So powerful was John's preaching, so strong was his renown and spirituality, that "the people were in expectation, and all men mused in their hearts of John, whether he were the Christ, or not." But John was quick to correct them: "I indeed baptize you with water; but one mightier than I cometh, the latchet of whose shoes I am not worthy to unloose: he shall baptize you with the Holy Ghost and with fire" (Luke 3:15–16). John was careful to draw a clear distinction between himself and the Messiah, between the things that he could do and what the Messiah would do. "He . . . is mightier than I" was John's repeated message (Matthew 3:11).

Soon John's followers noticed, with a twinge of resentment, that Jesus was now starting to baptize "and all men come to him." John reminded them: "He that hath the bride is the bridegroom: but the friend of the bridegroom, which standeth and heareth him, rejoiceth greatly because of the bridegroom's voice: this my joy therefore is fulfilled. He must increase, but I must decrease" (John 3:26, 29–30).

Think about it: John could have puffed himself up, thought himself superior to others, and boasted of his ministry and mission. After all, he had baptized the Son of God! He could have taken glory to himself and felt entitled to special recognition and treatment. Instead, what we know of John speaks of his humility, sincerity, and consecration. He seemed to know his place and simply desired to perform his duties in a way that brought glory and honor to God. Rather than taking credit for his own successes, he said, "A man can receive nothing, except it be given him from heaven" (John 3:27). His attitude was not "Pay attention to me" but rather "Behold the Lamb of God, which taketh away the sin of the world" (John 1:29). John the Baptist was humble.

LESS THAN THE DUST

Why is it so hard to be like John the Baptist? Why is pride such a common problem—as President Ezra Taft Benson called it, "the universal sin"?[17] Why does the smallest success so quickly lead us to overestimate our own talents and assume that we are better than others (see D&C 121:39)? And why does an accomplishment by someone else so easily lead to envy and bitterness?

Mormon wrote movingly of the prideful tendency of man:

"O how foolish, and how vain . . . are the children of men . . . ! Yea, how quick to be lifted up in pride; yea, how quick to boast, . . . and how slow are they to remember the Lord their God, and to give ear to his counsels . . . ! O how great is the nothingness of the children of men; yea, even they are less than the dust of the earth" (Helaman 12:4–5, 7).

Mormon went on to observe that the dust, the hills and mountains, even the earth itself obey God's every command (see Helaman 12:8–17). Why can't His children be more like that?

Maybe part of the reason is the innate, deep-seated urge we all have to pursue excellence. We all know, deep in our hearts, that even though we "were created of the dust" (Mosiah 2:25), we are destined for something greater: we are meant to learn and grow and progress. But with the ambition to work hard and achieve comes the risk that we will attribute to ourselves any advancements we make and forget our dependence on God.

"When they are learned they think they are wise," Jacob noted, "and they hearken not unto the counsel of God, for they set it aside, supposing they know of themselves, wherefore, their wisdom is foolishness and it profiteth them not. And they shall perish. But to be learned is good if they hearken unto the counsels of God" (2 Nephi 9:28–29). To achieve and to work hard, to be successful and to be learned, all are good *if* we hearken unto the counsels of God. The key is that two-letter word *if,* for *if* we truly hearken unto God, we will humbly follow His counsel and do His will.

The problem isn't in trying to learn and grow and become something greater; it's in trying "to become something without God. We may try in many ways to prove our worth by seeking wealth, power, or praise of men. Yet, when we can finally admit that we are nothing without God, the Savior invites us to lay on the altar the great burden of trying to do everything on our own or of assuming more responsibility than we have."[18]

In essence, this is what it means to be humble and holy—not wallowing in our worthlessness but acknowledging our dependence on the Lord. The humble accept His invitation to follow Him and become like Him. In their hunger for greatness—not worldly praise but the approval of God—they draw on the Lord's strength and His solutions. As James taught, "Humble yourselves in the sight of the Lord, and he shall lift you up" (James 4:10).

Consider the example of Jesus Christ. Though clearly a man of great power, He readily acknowledged: "I can of mine own self do nothing. . . . I seek not mine own will, but the will of the Father which hath sent me" (John 5:30). He never lost sight of the Source of His power. Knowing the real source of power is a central principle for all who hold the priesthood of God and seek with all their heart to become holy men of God.

THE BLESSINGS OF HUMILITY

In recent years, the idea of humility has been getting renewed attention in—of all places—the hard-hitting business world. Several large, successful corporations have begun to prize humble leaders over the brash, overbearing kind. Humble leaders, they've found, "listen well, admit mistakes, and share the limelight."[19] They have helping hearts; they encourage teamwork and promote collaboration. They see themselves not as kings who issue orders but as coworkers in a worthwhile endeavor. Humble leaders see themselves authentically, with both strengths and weaknesses, and they recognize that leading others and serving them are not mutually exclusive efforts. One can be visionary and relentless, with the mind of a leader, and still be humble and teachable, with the heart of a servant.

Company executives are finding that when they hire leaders who are humble and eager to improve, the entire company benefits. A culture of humility and cooperation spreads throughout the workforce, bringing out the best in everyone.

If this attitude can improve the corporate world, think about what it could do for our interactions in our homes and communities. Imagine what might happen if we priesthood holders listened a little better, admitted our errors, stopped worrying about who gets credit, and were just a little more patient and loving. Humility just may be the key that unlocks the door to stronger organizations, improved relations, and happier lives, marriages, and families.

Think of these additional blessings of a humble approach to life:

The humble are less likely to lose hope when things go wrong or when they fall short, because they aren't depending on their own power to overcome such failures. They trust that the Lord's grace is sufficient to make weak things strong (see Ether 12:27).

The humble are more likely to see divine purpose and learning opportunities in their setbacks.

The humble can always ask for help, and they don't insist on that help coming in their way or on their timetable.

The humble have a sensitive conscience and are quick to repent. Often, this also makes them sympathetic toward the weaknesses of others and therefore quick to forgive.

Like God, the humble are no respecter of persons. They recognize the value of others because they see them as fellow children of God.

Because they see God as the inexhaustible source of all good things—for themselves and for others—the humble never worry that this goodness will run out. They don't assume that good fortune for one person means less of it for themselves. Consequently, they are less likely to be resentful when a gift or blessing is given to someone else.

The humble are thankful and quick to express gratitude to

God and others. This is why humble people tend to be happy. In fact, because they are able to rejoice not only in their own blessings but also in the blessings of others, their reasons to rejoice are greatly multiplied.

The humble have a deeper capacity to love and serve. They love without measure. Because their hearts are not crowded with envy, they are free to genuinely care about others. Because they are not threatened by another's success, they are free to help others succeed and authentically love them.

The humble happily serve others, even if their service goes unnoticed. They are really serving God, after all, and they know that He is aware of their efforts.

CHOOSING HUMILITY

Of course we would all like to enjoy these blessings. But how do we get there? How do we become more humble?

President Spencer W. Kimball offered this counsel: "How does one get humble? To me, one must constantly be reminded of his dependence. On whom dependent? On the Lord."[20] The question for us is how we will be reminded of our dependence on the Lord. Can we constantly remind ourselves, or will we need reminders from our trials and our circumstances?

The scriptures seem to indicate that these are the two main paths to humility—we can choose to be humble, or we can be compelled to be humble. And one of these paths is

BE HUMBLE

much more pleasant than the other. Here are the words Alma used: "A man sometimes, if he is compelled to be humble, seeketh repentance. . . . Do ye not suppose that they are more blessed who truly humble themselves because of the word? . . . Yea, he that truly humbleth himself, and repenteth of his sins, and endureth to the end, the same shall be blessed—yea, much more blessed than they who are compelled to be humble. . . . Therefore, blessed are they who humble themselves without being compelled to be humble" (Alma 32:13–16).

That doesn't mean that choosing humility will be easy. Benjamin Franklin learned this long ago. In his autobiography, Franklin told of his strong desire to develop a worthy character. To accomplish his goal, he made a list of the twelve virtues he most wanted to achieve and then came up with a systematic plan to practice each one. After learning of the plan, a friend suggested that he add one more virtue to his list, one that many felt he needed. Franklin agreed, and he added humility.[21] Later in life, Benjamin Franklin wrote that it was the virtue of humility that allowed him to have such great influence for good.

As St. Augustine said: "Do you wish to rise? Begin by descending. You plan a tower that will pierce the clouds? Lay first the foundation of humility."[22]

While it may seem that certain people are naturally humbler than others, the fact is that humility is not the exclusive possession of any particular class or type of people. It can be found among the rich and the poor of any race or nationality. That is because true humility is a conscious choice. Anyone can choose to be humble. Similarly, anyone can choose to be prideful. Even those who face humbling circumstances retain their right to choose resentment and bitterness. Yes, even when life compels us to be humble, humility remains a choice that we alone can make.

And it's a choice we must continue to make throughout our lives. That's because of a quirky characteristic of humility: as soon as you think you have it, you probably don't. On the other hand, the humblest people tend to be those who feel they still have a long way to go. In *The Screwtape Letters,* C. S. Lewis's imaginative conversation between two devils, one of the devils notes with concern that a man they are trying to deceive is developing humility. The devil suggests to his associate a solution: "Your patient has become humble; have you drawn his attention to the fact?"[23]

Humility does not, however, mean constantly dwelling on our weaknesses and failures and denying our successes. President Dieter F. Uchtdorf expressed it well: "We don't discover humility by thinking less *of* ourselves; we discover humility by thinking less *about* ourselves."[24]

If you can make *that* choice, and keep making it throughout your life, then you are likely well on your way to developing humility as a habit of holiness.

STONE OF HELP

Some 3,000 years ago, during a time of great conflict, Samuel the prophet led ancient Israel to victory over a powerful enemy. Samuel placed a large stone at the place of their deliverance and dedicated it as a monument to God's assistance. He called the stone Ebenezer, which means "stone of help." The stone became a symbol of the Lord's goodness and strength.

This practice of raising memorials to divine help has deep roots in ancient Israel. Generations earlier, after the Israelites crossed the mighty Jordan River on dry ground and entered the promised land, their leader, Joshua, commanded the people to gather twelve stones from the river and build a monument. He explained that the purpose of the monument was to build faith in future generations, that "when [their] children ask . . . in time to come, saying, What mean ye by these stones?" they could tell their children how the Lord helped them in their hour of need (see Joshua 4:1–7).

Many centuries later, in 1749, twenty-three-year-old Robert Robinson wrote the beloved hymn "Come, Thou Fount of Every Blessing." He referenced the biblical Ebenezer stone when he wrote:

> *Here I raise my Ebenezer;*
> *Hither by Thy help I've come.*
> *And I hope, by Thy good pleasure,*
> *Safely to arrive at home.*

Once a prodigal who wandered in rebelliousness and sin, Robinson remembered his own divine rescue, which had led him to turn his life around. So it was from personal experience that he wrote:

> *Streams of mercy, never ceasing,*
> *Call for songs of loudest praise.*

Those who have felt divine mercy seem to sing the most fervent songs of praise. Their change of heart continually reminds them of the grace they've received.

Life is full of rivers to cross, full of challenges to overcome. However, those who live with a heart of humility and an eye of faith understand that they did not cross their rivers alone, nor will they cross tomorrow's rivers successfully without divine help. In a way, each of us could raise an Ebenezer of hope, a monument of faith, a memorial to the heavenly favor and forgiveness extended to us. We could recall God's love and kindness, His help and healing, His victory over despair and hopelessness in our own souls. It may not be a monument of stone—indeed, hearts filled with humility and gratitude are the most meaningful memorials. Whatever form our memorial takes, acknowledging the help we've received renews our hope that by His good pleasure and in His due time, we will safely arrive at home.

Chapter Six

BE PATIENT

I n 1833, the poet and priest John Henry Newman was traveling from Europe back to his home in England. He was already ill and homesick when he was seized by an attack of malaria. To make matters worse, the easterly breezes stopped blowing, thick fog closed in, and his ship was stalled at sea. He longed for England—for home—and became frustrated at the delay. Being stationary at sea can be as difficult as being tossed by the sea.

In these circumstances, Newman's heart turned heavenward. He was discouraged and needed divine comfort and assurance. He was weary and needed strength and sustenance. He was enshrouded in fog and the darkness of despair and needed heaven's light.[25] During those days while becalmed at sea, Newman wrote the words for which he would long be remembered—words we still sing today:

Lead, kindly Light, amid th'encircling gloom;
Lead thou me on!
The night is dark, and I am far from home;
Lead thou me on!
Keep thou my feet;
I do not ask to see the distant scene—
    one step enough for me.[26]

There's something about human nature that longs to see the distant scene. Maybe it's pride or fear or indecision, but whatever it is, we hesitate to take another step unless we know exactly where it leads. We want to plot our whole path, complete with milestones along the way. While goal-setting and planning are important for growth and progress, the fact is that we can't see far off—at least, not the way God can. As John Henry Newman learned, life is just as much about patience and trust as it is about assertiveness and self-confidence.

No matter how good our long-term plans might be, life is lived patiently, one step at a time.

For many of us, life's most difficult trials are found not in dramatic tragedies that require heroic action but in the mundane, day-to-day tests of endurance that require patience. We can't always get the ship of life moving by our own resourcefulness and initiative. Sometimes we just have to wait, to stay awhile in life's present moments, to see them through patiently till the end. During those seasons of life, inspiration and beauty can be born, faith in everlasting things can be rekindled and strengthened, and steadfastness and commitment to truth can be deepened. We can take comfort in the words of the Psalmist: "Wait on the Lord: be of good courage, and he shall strengthen thine heart" (Psalm 27:14). The Lord tells us that He will try the faith and the patience of His people (see Mosiah 23:21). As Elder Neal A. Maxwell taught, "Since faith in the timing of the Lord may be tried, let us learn to say not only, 'Thy will be done,' but patiently also, 'Thy timing be done.'"[27]

Perhaps it shouldn't surprise us that the God of Heaven, who is from all eternity to all eternity, is a God of patience and long-suffering. Nor should we be shocked to learn that God wants us to develop this holy habit in our efforts to become like Him. Indeed, we will never truly understand the workings of the Spirit and ways of the Lord without patience.

WHAT PATIENCE IS—AND WHAT IT IS NOT

Thinking of patience as an attribute of godliness and a habit of holiness helps us understand what patience really is. Patience does not mean miserably suffering in silence while we wait to get what we want—that's more like impatience! Nor is patience shoulder-shrugging indifference. God is patient, but He is hardly apathetic. Patience is active, not passive, and it calls upon the very strength of the soul. Patience is focused action, for those who are patient have learned to distinguish between things they can control and things they cannot.

Patience does not merely wait for the passing of time to make everything better. Rather, the patience we're talking about is alive and invigorating—the kind the Apostle Paul described as "patient continuance in well doing" (Romans 2:7).

President Dieter F. Uchtdorf explained: "Patience means accepting that which cannot be changed and facing it with courage, grace, and faith. It means being 'willing to submit to all things which the Lord seeth fit to inflict upon [us], even as a child doth submit to his father' (Mosiah 3:19). Ultimately, patience means being 'firm and steadfast, and immovable in keeping the commandments of the Lord' (1 Nephi 2:10) every hour of every day, even when it is hard to do so."[28]

This is why patient people seem serene and undisturbed by things like bad weather, bad traffic, or bad moods of people around them. Instead, they calmly focus on doing what they can—everything they can—and they never give up, even if the results they seek are a long time in coming.

Patience requires an eternal perspective—this is why God is so patient. With such a perspective, patient people kindly and lovingly allow others (and themselves) the time they need to reach their full potential. They resist putting undue pressure and unrealistic expectations on others, knowing that would only hinder growth and create frustration.

Patience means not despairing when mistakes happen. When patient people are offended, they don't feed the resentment or anger; instead, they work out a solution. Patience inspires us to give people another chance and the benefit of the doubt, just as we hope they will do for us.

We need patience in all aspects of life, but perhaps we can explore just two in which patience is particularly needful: in our times of suffering and in our efforts to improve our lives. In fact, it turns out that patience in one fosters patience in the other.

PATIENT IN SUFFERING

The pathway of life has never been a smooth, scenic expressway. Obstacles, roadblocks, and rough patches are part of everyone's journey. Some of these are small enough that we can avoid them or simple enough that we can quickly find solutions. There are other times when we simply have to buckle up, hold on for dear life, and ride it out. Some troubles are unavoidable and have no easy solutions. In those cases, the best we can do is to face those troubles head-on and keep moving in a positive direction.

But then there are situations in which the best thing might be to patiently wait it out. Such situations might be less like a rough road that simply has to be crossed and more like a riptide—a powerful current that runs beneath the surface of the ocean. A few years ago, a friend was caught in a riptide that could have cost him his life. He discovered that if he tried to swim the most direct route to the shore, the riptide kept dragging him back out to sea. It didn't matter how hard he tried (and he was a strong swimmer); the more furiously he swam against the riptide, the more it seemed to pull him in the other direction, draining his strength in the process. In this case, the best solution was not to attack the problem head on but to swim parallel to the beach until he came to a safe area away from the riptide. Only then could he begin to head for the shore.

As you can imagine, when a riptide is trying to pull you out to sea, it's very hard to resist the urge to swim as quickly as possible to the shore. But resisting that urge is the only way to survive. Some of life's trials are like that. We simply have to wait patiently for certain things to pass, relying in the meantime on the Lord to sustain us until we reach safety.[29]

My dear mother[30] learned about her own resilience when her beloved husband died, followed shortly thereafter by brain surgery and serious health problems of her own. She was a widow and in a wheelchair for more than thirty years, and yet, uncomplainingly, she viewed each day as a gift and an opportunity to love and care. The string of difficulties she endured seemed unending, but she just carried on—one hour, one day, one week at a time. It wasn't easy, but it became a little easier with the passing of time as she patiently, lovingly endured. She spoke many times to her posterity of her gratitude to God for the blessings of life and bore powerful witness of the many tender mercies given to her during her life. Even in her long period of faithful endurance, she patiently waited upon the Lord and trusted His purposes and promises. Grounding herself in her faith in the Savior and the hope of a joyful eternity with her beloved husband, she was able to face years of heartache and suffering with a serenity and strength that bolstered and comforted her family. Her positive influence and strength of character and testimony resounds throughout our family still today.

That's the other hidden blessing of suffering: those experiences that seem to be weakening us are actually, in many cases, not only revealing our strength but also increasing it. As the Apostle Paul taught, "We glory in tribulations also: knowing that tribulation worketh patience" (Romans 5:3).

Isn't that interesting? Tribulations *require* patience, but at the same time they also *teach us* patience. They prompt us to develop a more hopeful view by cultivating friendships with positive people. They move us to challenge our negative thoughts and strive for a larger perspective. They can even inspire us to reach out to others in love and kindness, which always helps us feel better. Ultimately, patiently bearing up under trials will develop in us the strength and resilience we will need for the next trial. That seems to be the Lord's way of helping us when we struggle; rather than removing the burdens on our backs, He strengthens our backs, as He did for Alma's people in the Book of Mormon: "The Lord did strengthen them that they could bear up their burdens with ease, and they did submit cheerfully and with patience to all the will of the Lord" (Mosiah 24:15).

John Henry Newman was right: sometimes one step has to be enough, because that is all we are given. We don't see the future; we can't foretell how our trials will be resolved. But we go ahead and take that next step because we have faith that there is a resolution up ahead somewhere. Abraham Lincoln said it this way: "The best thing about the future is that it only comes one day at a time." Over time—one day, one step at a time—people *can* heal from life's inevitable trials and tribulations. The healing journey is different for each person. It follows no set time frame or pattern. It's a time to exercise great patience with others and with ourselves.

"LET PATIENCE HAVE HER PERFECT WORK" (JAMES 1:4)

For many years my sons and I served as home teachers to a man who makes his living as a potter.[31] He is an artist of clay, and he speaks lovingly of his craft, which he developed over many, many years of training and experience. Pottery is among mankind's oldest and most enduring art forms. The process itself feels like a work of art, as the expert potter carefully, patiently shapes a lump of lifeless clay into a beautiful vessel. While finishing the work takes time and patient effort, and can sometimes be a little messy, the result is clearly worth it.

It's no wonder that pottery-making is often used as a

metaphor for how our lives are gently molded by the patient hand of God: "Behold, as the clay is in the potter's hand, so are ye in mine hand," the Lord told Jeremiah (Jeremiah 18:6).

It has been said that each of us is a masterpiece in progress. That may seem trite or clichéd, but it's a reassuring thought during those disheartening times when we feel like anything but a masterpiece—times when we may feel like giving up.

A masterpiece is a work that demonstrates extraordinary talent, artistic skill, or workmanship—a supreme intellectual or artistic achievement. Historically, a masterpiece represented an artist's finest piece of work, evidence that he or she, after years of perfecting a craft, had achieved the rank of master. Yet when we see or read or listen to a masterpiece, we rarely think of the time, the effort—even the mistakes—that accompanied its creation.

That's good to remember not only as we consider our personal growth and development but also as we interact with others whom the Master Potter is patiently molding and shaping. If we can patiently allow the Master Potter to do His work, we will see a beautiful result.

The Epistle of James encourages us to "let patience have her perfect work" (James 1:4).[32] When it comes to our family relationships, even when we do our best to "train up a child in the way he should go," sometimes the promise that "he will not depart from it" is not fulfilled until "he is old" (Proverbs 22:6). Trying to shortcut this process of patient change by using coercion or undue pressure is like pulling on a sapling to get it to grow faster. Trees don't grow that way, and neither do people. In our roles as fathers and as priesthood leaders, patience and kindness are always better than force and fury. When we expect too much and try too hard to change people, we show a lack of confidence and patience in the transforming power of God's word and in the critical role of the Holy Ghost. Maybe that's why "long-suffering" comes right after "persuasion" in the Lord's formula for effective priesthood leadership (see D&C 121:41). When we impatiently try to put another person's growth on our schedule instead of theirs, we risk violating his or her agency, and we may be doing more harm than good.[33]

Patience is the loving restraint with which we watch a child try a new task, and try again and again. Patience with others is a form of charity, a loving willingness to wait, to allow growth and change. Patience is holding back and waiting with love and compassion. When we show faith that improvement will come, children and loved ones can begin to blossom with hope. When we shed the love and light of sincere patience and compassion upon others, they can feel empowered to change for the better. Patience is giving power to others and letting them grow at their own pace.

All beautiful gardens began as patches of soil, and became glorious only because someone was willing to wait and willing to nurture with love. No beautiful garden or masterpiece is ever created all at once, and none will ever thrive if neglected. So be thankful for the small successes, the simple joys, the good times, and even the hard times. Each one is another brushstroke, another stanza, another note toward the finished product. Each one gives us experience, teaches us, and strengthens us for what lies ahead. Life is a process of change and improvement: becoming a little kinder, a little better, a little holier. So be patient with the process in others and in yourself, and remember that each of us is a work in progress—a masterpiece in the making.

Consider this wise counsel from President Dieter F. Uchtdorf: "God wants to help us to eventually turn all of our weaknesses into strengths, but He knows that this is a long-term goal."[34] We need a broader perspective and more self-compassion as we work to become more patient. That also means that perhaps we need to ease up a little on ourselves. Expecting perfection right now—of ourselves and others—leads to frustration and discouragement.

Nobel Prize winner Albert Einstein said of his work, "It's not that I'm so smart, it's just that I stay with problems longer."[35] Patience doesn't make the problems go away, but as we've all witnessed and experienced, there's power in patience that makes us equal to the task. Like Einstein, lifelong learners and growers know that great patience is needed in their quest for learning and growth.

True, we might not revolutionize the world with

remarkable inventions or amazing achievements, but we can bless our posterity with an example of patience and perseverance, an attitude of devotion to principle, a desire to be true to the truth, a sincere yearning to be holy men of God. We might not achieve prominence in the eyes of the world, but we can conquer the natural man by patiently persevering in worthy causes. We can preside in our homes as honorable priesthood holders with love and righteousness. We thereby become, in time, the Master Potter's greatest masterpiece.

Chapter Seven

BE FULL OF LOVE

President Harold B. Lee spoke openly about his feelings of inadequacy when he was sustained as the eleventh President of the Church. He credited his counselors in the First Presidency and the gifts of the Spirit with giving him the strength to carry such a huge burden.

In the April 1973 general conference, he spoke of the importance of loving God and the people you serve: "As I come to you at the closing moments of this conference, I would like to take you back now to just one incident, and I am sorry that I can tell you only a part of it because of the limitations of some things contained therein.

"It was just before the dedication of the Los Angeles Temple. We were all preparing for that great occasion. It was something new in my life, when along about three or four o'clock in the morning, I enjoyed an experience that I think was not a dream, but it must have been a vision. It seemed that I was witnessing a great spiritual gathering, where men and women were standing up, two or three at a time, and speaking in tongues. The spirit was so unusual. I seemed to have heard the voice of President David O. McKay say, 'If you want to love God, you have to learn to love and serve the people. That is the way you show your love for God.' And there were other things then that I saw and heard."[36]

To love God and to love people, all people, is essential for a holy life. As we strive to fill our soul with love, we will have less room in our heart for fear (see Moroni 8:16), for anger (see Moroni 9:5), or for jealousy (see D&C 88:123).

CHARITY IS HOLY LOVE

Charity is defined beautifully as "the pure love of Christ" (Moroni 7:47). Charity is not just love; it is the holy love possessed by the Savior—pure, divine, eternal, selfless, and freely offered to others through compassionate service. This definition of charity far exceeds generous feelings or the kind but limited act of simply giving to those in need. It is significantly more than that. Charity is a powerful spiritual gift that we should seek with all our heart.

Elder Jeffrey R. Holland taught: "True charity, the absolutely pure, perfect love of Christ, has really been known only once in this world—in the form of Christ Himself, the Son of the living God. As in everything, Christ is the only one who got it all right, did it all perfectly, loved the way we are all to try to love. But even though we fall short, that divine standard is there for us. It is a goal toward which we are to keep reaching, keep striving—and, certainly, a goal to keep appreciating."[37]

UNDERSTANDING CHARITY

One way to look at the whole concept of charity is to divide it into three elements: first, how we make ourselves worthy to receive this great gift; second, the way the Lord provides the gift; and third, how we act once we receive the gift of charity.

1. The Apostle Paul makes some inspiring observations about charity in the thirteenth chapter of First Corinthians. He speaks of great acts of righteousness and declares that these are mostly worthless if they are not done with charity. Paul goes on to list many of the qualities of someone who is worthy of the gift of charity. The list includes being patient, kind, humble, courteous, unselfish, slow to anger, and sincere, among other fine qualities. As we practice and develop these Christlike attributes, we will become more worthy and the spiritual gift of charity will develop in our lives.

That may make it sound as though we need to be perfect before we can be charitable, but that's not the case. Even though "the Lord cannot look upon sin with the least degree of allowance" (Alma 45:16), in His tender mercy, He will bless us as we grow and keep trying to do what is right.

In another of his letters, Paul explains that as we "depart

from iniquity," we will become more useful to the Master and better prepared for His work. He compares us to vessels or household containers in a "great house" (2 Timothy 2:19–20). Some of the vessels are made of clay, some of wood, some of silver, and some of gold. The purer the vessel (with gold being the purest), the more honor is brought to the Master. Our task is to become a golden vessel—a worthy and valuable servant of the Lord.

One of the biggest obstacles to becoming a golden vessel is the immaturity of youth. So Paul counsels us to let go of our childish desires, to "follow righteousness, faith, charity, [and] peace, with them that call on the Lord out of a pure heart" (2 Timothy 2:22). Those striving to live a life of holiness must "put away childish things" (1 Corinthians 13:11) and seek after that which has eternal value. Children collect toys and sometimes seek new adventures at the expense of things that matter more, such as education, service to others, and developing personal character. The man of holiness is willing to delay gratification. He can still have fun and enjoy life, but he will see the world in a more mature way and will strive to serve others and make a lasting contribution. In order to receive the most valuable spiritual gifts (and Paul says that charity is among the greatest), we must do our best to seek holiness by refining ourselves, ridding ourselves of impurity, and becoming useful vessels, or servants, of the Lord (see 1 Corinthians 13:13).

BE FULL OF LOVE

2. As we become holier, more worthy vessels, the Lord will begin to fill us with His love (see Moroni 7:48). That is another element in the development of the spiritual gift of charity: we will begin to feel love for those around us like we have never felt it before. It might begin with family members and good friends, but as charity blossoms in our heart, feelings of love will spread to people we don't even know. When you are a worthy vessel and your love for the Lord and His children begins to fill your very soul, you know you are receiving more of the gift of charity.

3. As the Lord fills His worthy servants with His love, their love deepens and grows into a love we can call holy. This kind of love seems to come naturally to us when we seek it and are worthy of it. It feels right and brings great joy. As this love expands and fills us, it begins to overflow into the world around us in compassionate service. This is the third element of charity: compassion.

The four Gospels of the New Testament frequently refer to the Lord's compassion on those He met.[38] These feelings of compassion seem to come out of His pure love for the people. Deeds of compassion are love brought to action. If we do not act upon the love we feel in compassionate service to others, then our charity is not complete.

To summarize, the three elements of charity are (1) being a worthy vessel, (2) allowing pure love to fill our souls, and (3) acting upon that love in compassionate service. This is a simple formula, but like all aspects of holiness, it takes a lifetime and more to fully achieve.

LOVE FOR OUR NEIGHBORS

Although holiness is a personal virtue, it can be fully attained and practiced only in the company of others. It is in community that we put into action the behaviors that typify a holy life. Isolation may remove the distractions of the world and empower the contemplative elements of holiness, but the complete manifestation of holiness must include action rooted in compassionate service.

In His relationships with others, Jesus was the perfect example of true communal charity. He mingled freely with the communities surrounding Jerusalem and even ventured into the Samaritan villages looked down upon by the Jews (see John 4:40). As He recognized the spiritual and physical needs of the people, He was "moved with compassion" (Matthew 9:36) and performed healing and blessing miracles in their behalf.

All around us are those who live in need. For some, the nature of the difficulty is obvious. Others carry a burden that may not be evident but is nonetheless hard to bear. As we pay close attention to the people about us, we will become aware of their suffering and how we can help lighten the load they carry.

The recipient of our love may be someone to whom we are close or one who crosses our path for only a moment. Developing charity will prepare us to act in the instant of opportunity to do all we can. And the good we do may be just what is needed.

The light of our lives burns brighter and all the world seems better when we give a little love to assist someone in need. And in such service, we also serve the One who inspires it—for, said He, "Inasmuch as ye have done it unto one of the least of these . . . , ye have done it unto me" (Matthew 25:40).

SELF-COMPASSION IS ESSENTIAL TO HOLINESS

We speak of holiness as the result of putting off the natural man, or overcoming the carnal self (see Mosiah 3:19). This is true, of course, but it is important not to see the pursuit of holiness as a battle with yourself. Our Creator has, in a manner of speaking, hardwired us as carnal beings. The natural man plays a vital role in our development. Often, he represents the opposition that is an essential part of the mortal journey (see 2 Nephi 2:11–12). Rather than feeling a need to suppress the natural man, think of yourself as making efforts to transcend and positively exceed the inclinations of your carnal nature. The adage "Hate the sin but love the sinner" should be applied to yourself as well as to others.

The fact that you are reading this book likely means you are interested in understanding and practicing greater holiness. Given your spiritual inclinations, your self-esteem or self-confidence should be high, and justifiably so. However, self-esteem can be fickle, because it is often based largely on comparison with others or a notion of how we are perceived by those around us. One minute we may be feeling like a superstar and the next, messages we receive from our environment (including our own self-talk) can leave us feeling far less than adequate. This is natural, especially when we are entering a new phase of life where the learning curve may be quite steep. It is also to be expected that, even when we've done our best, we will experience some downright failures. Hopefully these won't be catastrophic, but despite the positives connected with failure, our self-esteem may take a serious hit and leave us feeling somewhat worthless and hopeless.

Much of this roller coaster of self-esteem can be avoided, however, if we stop focusing on how well we think we are doing at the moment and treat ourselves with the same love and tolerance we try so hard to afford others.

The Savior gave us a clue about managing self-esteem when He said, "Let every man esteem his brother as himself, and practise virtue and holiness before me" (D&C 38:24). Then, repeating Himself as a matter of special emphasis, He said, "And again I say unto you, let every man esteem his brother as himself" (D&C 38:25). Generally, when we read those scriptures we focus on the phrase *esteem his brother* without considering that the Lord said emphatically that we must esteem or love *ourselves* with equal respect and regard. In fact, it may well be that our ability to love others is directly related to our ability to love ourselves, and the level of tolerance we have for others and the depth of our concern for others is dependent upon harboring similar feelings for ourselves.

Once when my wife and I were in the kitchen cooking together,[39] I tried to pick up a bottle of salad dressing, and it slipped out of my fingers and spilled on the counter. Immediately the words sprang to my mind, *You idiot!* Almost as quickly, my wife said to me, "Oh, that's OK. I'll just wipe it up."

Now, if my wife had spilled the dressing, would I have yelled, "You idiot!" at her? Of course not! I would have had much more compassion for her than that. Why, then, did it seem fine for me to say that to myself? Why did I not respond to myself with the compassionate words she had used to make me feel better? At that moment, at least, my level of self-compassion was quite low.

As President Dieter F. Uchtdorf said, "Many of you are endlessly compassionate and patient with the weaknesses of others. Please remember also to be compassionate and patient with yourself."[40]

We often talk to ourselves in a critical and demeaning manner we would be very unlikely to use with anyone else, even someone we don't like very much. Such self-talk is as damaging to our holiness as it would be if we were talking to someone else.

Dr. Kristen Neff, an associate professor at the University

of Texas at Austin, has said, "With self-compassion, we give ourselves the same kindness and care we'd give to a good friend."[41] Wouldn't our lives be better if we cared for ourselves as if we liked ourselves?

Dr. Neff suggests that an appropriate level of self-compassion may be realized when we approach ourselves with an attitude of:

Self-kindness—Caring for ourselves, not in a selfish way, but just as we would a good friend or loved one. Remember, our ability to love others is highly correlated with our ability to love ourselves.

Mindfulness—Developing an awareness of our own mental state and accepting our feelings for what they are without harsh judgment.

Common humanity—We are all mortal beings in a common experience full of challenges and frequent errors. Add to that our knowledge that we are all—*all of us*—children of God the Father. We deserve love and respect, even from ourselves.

A fascinating story unfolds in the Old Testament as the children of Israel are weakening in their faith and complaining of their hardships. In order to bring them to remembrance, the Lord sent among them poisonous serpents whose bite was fatal. When the people were adequately humbled and desperately in need of rescue, Moses was commanded to make a serpent of brass and raise it on a pole for all to see. Those who would focus their attention on the brazen serpent were healed from the venomous bite (see Numbers 21:4–9). This is where the Old Testament account ends.

Additional insight is provided by Alma in the Book of Mormon. He taught that the brazen serpent was a type of the Savior, for all who look to Him will live. But Alma also indicates that while many who were bitten by the snakes "did look and live, . . . there were many who were so hardened that they would not look, therefore they perished" (Alma 33:19–20).

We might ask why, when dying of poison and with evidence that a cure was readily available, would anyone not look? Alma offered this explanation: "Now the reason they would not look is because they did not believe that it would heal them" (Alma 33:20). Consider Alma's words with this emphasis added: "Now the reason they would not look is because they did not believe that it would heal *them.*" Perhaps they knew there was healing power in the representation of their Lord, but they could not accept that His grace might be applied to *them.* It seems their hearts were hardened against themselves, and it led to their demise.

It is easy to believe the Lord loves others, hears their prayers, and blesses them. It is sometimes more difficult to feel that we deserve the attention of the Master. As bearers of the priesthood, we know it is easier to give a priesthood blessing than it is to ask for one ourselves. As we learn to care for ourselves and humbly recognize our need for help, we will be the recipients of the kinds of blessings we seek for others.

At the beginning of a demanding work assignment, I was feeling far less than adequate.[42] There was such a steep learning curve! A respected colleague stopped me in the hallway one day and said, "Do you want to know how to succeed in your assignment?" I responded with an anxious yes. The advice: "Never make a mistake." The counsel was given in jest, but I certainly thought there was some truth to it.

Of course, I didn't always live up to that lofty standard, but I did learn that as a regular mortal prone to error, and working daily with men and women I admired and who had high expectations for my efforts, I couldn't let something as capricious as self-esteem determine my attitude or behavior. Great peace comes in realizing that our inherent value as children of God remains unchanged even when we make mistakes. In most cases, when you're acting like your own worst enemy, you're probably your *only* enemy.

In your quest for holiness, don't forget to soften your heart toward yourself. Cultivate a healthy self-love that is not dependent on the fickle superficiality of self-image or self-esteem. Life offers many learning opportunities by which we can refine and internalize a profound level of self-compassion that will allow us to be kind and understanding of ourselves through the ups and downs, the rough landings, and even the occasional crashes of life.

Becoming holy is a lifelong and into-the-eternities process. Only the Savior achieved perfect holiness as a mortal being, and He had a big head start! Incorporating the habits of holiness into your life, including a heart full of divine love, should bring joy and a profound sense of gratitude for the privilege of trying, failing, and trying again without the impossible pressure of being in a single-elimination tournament. Crowds on both sides of the veil are rooting for you, and you have the Father, your Elder-Brother Savior, and the Holy Spirit as your personal coaches, always available through prayerful consultation. The power is in you; you were born with it. True holiness is within your reach.

Chapter Eight

BE AS A CHILD

In early 1980, the First Presidency announced the second World Conference on Records. This important conference, stimulated by the success of Alex Haley's book *Roots,* was designed to encourage the preservation of records related to our individual and collective heritage. To get things started with a high level of enthusiasm, the First Presidency and other General Officers of the Church held a special meeting on the 26th floor of the Church Office Building in Salt Lake City. Employees of the Genealogy Department (now the Family History Department) were invited to the meeting, including myself.[43] President Spencer W. Kimball, who was the President of the Church at the time, presided.

As the meeting concluded, I made my way to the bank of elevators, pushed the button, and stood quietly waiting for an elevator to arrive. As with most tall buildings, the elevators

BE AS A CHILD

in the Church Office Building often take a while to reach the top level. In the meantime, President Kimball and the other meeting attendees started to gather by the elevators. Soon a bell sounded and a light came on above the elevator door right next to where I was standing. As the door opened, someone beckoned to President Kimball, courteously suggesting that he enter first with other members of the First Presidency and Quorum of the Twelve Apostles. As the President passed by me, he put his hand on mine and asked quietly, "Will you come?"

A bit shocked by his request, I simply responded, "Yes, sir." President Kimball then took me by the arm and led me into the elevator. There I stood, surrounded by General Authorities, with President Kimball clinging to my arm, our faces not ten inches apart. Out of respect, and feeling a bit intimidated, I gazed at the floor. President Kimball asked me a rather innocuous question, and I gave a quick response of some kind. It was then that I thought to myself, *I want to look into the eyes of the prophet.* With some trepidation, I lifted my head and looked directly into President Kimball's eyes, right into the windows of his soul. What I saw could be described only as pure love. I gazed for only a moment, but it was long enough to see the deep love the President had for me and for all of God's children.

Soon the elevator reached the bottom floor, and the Brethren exited to meet their next obligation. I returned to my office to contemplate the experience, but it wasn't until several days later that I really understood what I had seen in the eyes of the prophet.

It was a busy Saturday morning, and my wife and I were trying to accomplish the usual list of chores that had been put off until the weekend. Toward the end of the morning, our baby daughter let us know by her crying that she was hungry and needed some attention. The happy task fell to me, so I picked her up, put her in her high chair, and prepared some baby food. With the first taste of the fruity mix, her crying stopped. As I offered her another spoonful, my eyes met her upturned baby gaze. In her moist eyes was a look of pure love. "Those eyes," I said to myself. "I've seen them before." Then, in an instant, the elevator experience flashed through my mind, and an almost audible voice spoke, saying, "Except you become as a little child, you cannot enter into the kingdom of heaven" (see 3 Nephi 11:38).

I knew then the significance of what I had seen in the eyes of President Kimball. He had begun life as a pure and innocent child. He grew as a boy, worked as an adult, and struggled through all the usual vicissitudes of life. By great effort and consistent reliance upon Jesus Christ and His Atonement, President Kimball had become again innocent and full of pure love, like a child.

EXCEPT YE BECOME AS A CHILD

"The disciples [came] unto Jesus, saying, Who is the *greatest* in the kingdom of heaven? And Jesus called a little child unto him, and set him in the midst of them, and said, Verily I say unto you, Except ye be converted, and become as little *children*, ye shall not enter into the kingdom of heaven. Whosoever therefore shall *humble* himself as this little *child*, the same is greatest in the kingdom of heaven" (Matthew 18:1–4; emphasis added).

To be as a child is to love unconditionally. It is to accept others without prejudice or critical judgment, based on their inherent worth as children of God. Little children are naturally free from the learned paradigms and acquired behaviors that too quickly taint our view of mankind. Only when we overcome the suspicion and skepticism of the adult world can the light of pure love shine again in our eyes. All the habits of holiness are designed to assist in this essential process. Each one individually, and all of them collectively, when practiced with full purpose of heart and over many years of diligent persistence, trying and failing and trying again, will bring us once more to the sacred state of pure love and acceptance we all enjoyed as little children. It is in this Christlike state that we are prepared to enter again into the presence of the Lord, who showed us the way and prepared the path.

JESUS IS OUR HELPER

In Eastern Utah there is a little town called Helper. Perhaps it has seen better days, such as when it boomed as a mining and railroad town, but it remains home to a diverse and happy population. Helper was named after the "helper" locomotives that were added to the trains operated by the Denver and Rio Grande Western Railroad. The additional engines were necessary to power the trains over the steep grade of the mountain pass just west of the city.

Like those long and heavily loaded trains, we all are carrying wearisome burdens of one kind or another, some seen and some less obvious. On occasion, or maybe daily, we find ourselves at the bottom of a steep slope that taxes our physical and emotional strength. We need the extra push of a "helper." If we are willing to accept His help and recognize our childlike dependence, Jesus Christ will be our divine Helper. He is the ultimate source of strength and power. If we invite Him to join our struggle, we will find strength beyond our own and will have the determination and capacity to reach our personal potential as children of God.

WE ARE CHILDREN OF GOD, OUR FATHER

God is literally our Father. We are His children. To become as a little child is not to be childish, but childlike. Even the most mature, the wisest, and the best educated can bow before their Maker and, with a heart full of love and gratitude, seek to please Him and do His will. If we let Him, Heavenly Father can make more of our lives than we could ever do on our own. To submit to Him as a loving child is to avail ourselves of His all-knowing, all-powerful influence.

You may have heard the impressive story of a well digger and his young son. The man was working at the bottom of a deep well when his son arrived with lunch for him. The boy peered down into the well, but in the darkness of the deep hole he could not see his father. Finally, the son called down to him. When the man answered, his son prepared to drop the lunch sack down into the well, where his father could catch it. To the boy's surprise, his father called out, "Jump down into the well and share my lunch with me."

"Oh, Father," the boy replied, "the well is deep, and I can't see you in the darkness."

"It's OK," answered the father. "I can see you. Just jump and I'll catch you."

With some hesitation, but with great trust in his father, the boy jumped and was caught in his father's loving arms. That is the kind of childlike innocence and trust we should have in our Heavenly Father.

The innocence and purity of a child, joined with trust and confidence in a kind Father, will allow the magnanimous influence of heaven to bless our lives. Our outward appearance and circumstances may not dramatically change. Our flesh may not become like that of a newborn as did Naaman's.

We may have to give up some things we truly desire. But our heart will be renewed, and we will walk with greater peace and joy.

REMEMBER WHAT CHILDREN KNOW

This chapter on becoming as a child would not be complete without reference to Robert Fulghum's special insight on that subject. He wrote: "All I really need to know about how to live and what to do and how to be I learned in kindergarten. Wisdom was not at the top of the graduate-school mountain, but there in the sand pile at Sunday School." Fulghum then listed simple virtues that are often learned as a child, such as play fair, clean up your own mess, and don't take things that aren't yours.[44]

Add to that list several more things you can do even as a child:

- Say your prayers every day.
- Read the scriptures.
- Go to church on Sunday.
- Pay your tithing.
- Keep the Word of Wisdom.
- Tell your family you love them, and show them your love daily.
- You can probably think of more!

Holiness is best achieved in the context of childlike innocence, purity, faith, and trust. Indeed, "of such is the kingdom of God" (Mark 10:14). No man wants to sacrifice his manliness, nor should he, but the suppression of childlike qualities is not necessary to maintain manhood. Even in the toughest circumstances, when a man really needs to be a man, the childlike virtues of love and fairness, gentleness and strength, among many others, will serve him well.

Chapter Nine

CONCLUSION

Our definition of busyness changes as we get older, doesn't it? A teenager thinks that life simply cannot get any busier than it is right now. But ask that teenager's parents—or any couple with a young family—and they'll have something to say about just how hectic life can be. Some of us seem to run out of day before we run out of things to do. But others wait with little to do, watching the hands of the clock slowly go around the dial. Some don't have enough time; others seem to have too much.

Whatever our level of busyness, we all make daily choices about how we spend our time. In many cases, this can be a difficult decision—not because we lack good options but because we have so many. Too often, the enemy of the good is the good. We might feel overwhelmed with choices. What is most essential for us in life? How do we make sure we are putting first things first, that we are spending time on things that matter most? How can I be a better husband, father, son—a holier man?

Just as we try to nurture our physical and mental health, we need time for spiritual development—time to be holy. We enlarge our souls as we deeply ponder what God wants our lives to become, who He wants us to be. We expand our love for others and gain an understanding of what life is about as we turn to heaven in sincere prayer. We learn about God and about ourselves as His children as we read the scriptures and study carefully the words of living prophets. We become holier and put off the natural man as we are more submissive, meek, humble, and patient—as we develop the habits of holiness.

And every man who holds the priesthood of God has an additional reason to pursue these habits. With our ordination comes both the commission and the potential to become a little holier, a little more righteous, a little more in tune with the Spirit—a better man.

Holiness and heavenly things make earthly difficulties and trials bearable, even as they deepen joys and provide comfort and understanding. Turning our hearts to holiness is time well spent, time that can enhance our physical and mental health, our marriage and family relationships, and our overall sense of happiness and well-being. Taking time for holiness may be the most eternal and essential thing we do in life.

Just as life is not meant to be all fun and games, life is

not meant to be all prayer and meditation. We are to *live*—to interact, to work, to play and laugh, to go forward in the whole range of life's worthwhile endeavors. But time for holiness is not a distraction from life's purposes—*it is life* and the vital reason we are here: to draw closer to God and become more like Him.

Our Father in Heaven wants to share with us His joyous life and eternal splendor. He wants us to have "peace in this world, and eternal life in the world to come" (D&C 59:23). We are not pawns on some celestial chessboard, moving about under the capricious will of a stern and distant God. We are children of a loving Father. We are the focus of His greatest interest and yearning, and we are His greatest work and glory (see Moses 1:39). He really is our beloved and loving Father.

GRATITUDE AND HOLINESS

Our eternal quest as men of God is to become holy. The Lord said, "If you will that I give unto you a place in the celestial world, you must prepare yourselves by doing the things which I have commanded you and required of you" (D&C 78:7). What is required of us is to become holy even as He is (see 1 John 3:2–3; 3 Nephi 27:21, 27; Moroni 7:48). And that is the journey of eternity.

To become like Him is to know happiness, joy, peace, and eternal contentment. Indeed, the most godlike and holy people seem also to be the happiest. There are many reasons

CONCLUSION

for this, but one is surely the fact that the holier we become and the closer to God we are, the more clearly we see His hand in our lives and the more grateful we feel for His blessings. In other words, those who are grateful tend to be happier, and those who are happy tend to be more grateful. Happiness and gratitude simply go together. Scholars and scientists, poets and philosophers have connected them for generations. It's been said that gratitude makes sense of your past, brings peace for today, and creates a vision for tomorrow. Sincere gratitude is the fuel that generates growth and happiness and is the quality the Roman orator Cicero claimed was "not only the greatest of virtues, but the parent of all the others."[45]

We tend to think of gratitude primarily as a by-product of happiness—when life is good and things are going our way, we feel thankful. But this is only half of the truth. Those who choose to be grateful even during hard times discover that gratitude *creates* happiness. Gratitude to God for everything around us awakens wonder and awe; it stimulates kindness and affection; it deepens humility and creates space in the heart for love and warmth. Gratitude is not just a reaction to our quality of life—it is how we *determine* our quality of life. To be sure, happiness inspires gratitude, but gratitude also inspires happiness. Gratitude is found in every happy and holy person we know.

One of the greatest manifestations of holiness is an attitude of gratitude. So if we desire holiness, if we are discouraged and without hope, if we are overwhelmed and wonder where to begin, gratitude is a good place to start. Be sincerely grateful, and more holiness will come into your life. Holy men of God are grateful and "live in thanksgiving daily" (Alma 34:38).

We are grateful for you, dear reader, and our wish and hope for you is greater happiness and holiness as you journey through life.

NOTES

1. Bible Dictionary, "God."
2. A. W. Tozer, *The Pursuit of God* (Abbotsford, WI: Aneko Press, 2015).
3. See Elder Jeffrey R. Holland, General Conference Leadership Meeting, April 2017.
4. Robert L. Millet, *The Power of the Word* (Salt Lake City: Deseret Book, 1994), 73.
5. Carol F. McConkie, "The Beauty of Holiness," *Ensign,* May 2017.
6. Bruce C. Hafen, *A Disciple's Life: The Biography of Neal A. Maxwell* (Salt Lake City: Deseret Book, 2002), 110.
7. See, for example, the following general conference addresses: "Willing to Submit" (Apr. 1985), "For I Will Lead You Along" (Apr. 1988), "Murmur Not" (Oct. 1989), "Swallowed Up in the Will of the Father" (Oct. 1995), "Becometh as a Child" (Apr. 1996), "Content with the Things Allotted unto Us" (Apr. 2000), "Consecrate Thy Performance" (Apr. 2002).
8. See Hafen, *A Disciple's Life,* 14–15.

NOTES

9. Carrie A. Moore, *Deseret News*, July 28, 2004.
10. See Hafen, *A Disciple's Life,* 562.
11. "Willing to Submit," *Ensign*, May 1984.
12. "Joy and Spiritual Survival," *Ensign*, Nov. 2016.
13. "Swallowed Up in the Will of the Father," *Ensign*, Nov. 1995.
14. This story comes from the personal experience of Lloyd Newell.
15. Bruce R. McConkie, *Mormon Doctrine* (Salt Lake City: Bookcraft, 1958), 474.
16. "Meek=Weak, Right?" *LDS Positivity,* Dec. 22, 2011, positivity.obenchain.us/2011/12/22/meek-weak-right; spelling and punctuation standardized.
17. "Beware of Pride," *Ensign*, May 1989.
18. Catherine Thomas, "Blessed Are Ye," *Ensign*, June 1987.
19. Joann S. Lublin, "The Case for Humble Executives," *Wall Street Journal,* Oct. 20, 2015, wsj.com/articles/the-case-for-humble-executives-1445385076.
20. *The Teachings of Spencer W. Kimball* (Salt Lake City: Deseret Book, 1982), 233.
21. See *The Autobiography of Benjamin Franklin* (Philadelphia: Henry Altemus, 1895), 162–64.
22. In Everett L. Worthington Jr., *Humility: The Quiet Virtue* (West Conshohocken, PA: Templeton Press, 2007), 48.
23. *The Screwtape Letters* (San Francisco: HarperOne, 1982), 62–63.
24. "Pride and the Priesthood," *Ensign*, Nov. 2010.
25. See "Lead, Kindly Light," in Karen Lynn Davidson, *Our Latter-day Hymns: The Stories and the Messages* (Salt Lake City: Deseret Book, 1988), 126.
26. "Lead, Kindly Light," *Hymns* (1985), no. 97.
27. "Plow in Hope," *Ensign*, May 2001.
28. "Continue in Patience," *Ensign*, May 2010.

NOTES

29. See Merrilee Boyack, *In Trying Times, Just Keep Trying* (Salt Lake City: Deseret Book, 2010), 11.
30. This story comes from the personal experience of Lloyd Newell.
31. This story comes from the personal experience of Lloyd Newell.
32. Note that this verse comes right before the well-known verse that led Joseph Smith to the grove on an early spring morning in 1820.
33. See Jeffrey S. O'Driscoll and Hal B Gregersen, "'Persuasion and Love Unfeigned': The Exercise of Agency, Influence, and Principle," in *Joseph and Hyrum—Leading as One*, ed. Mark E. Mendenhall, Hal B Gregersen, Jeffrey S. O'Driscoll, Heidi S. Swinton, and Breck England (Provo, UT: Religious Studies Center, Brigham Young University; Salt Lake City: Deseret Book, 2010), 21–42.
34. Dieter F. Uchtdorf, "Forget Me Not," *Ensign*, Nov. 2011.
35. In Richard A. Singer Jr., *Your Daily Walk with the Great Minds: Wisdom and Enlightenment of the Past and Present* (Ann Arbor, MI: Loving Healing Press, 2006), 4.
36. *Ensign*, May 1973.
37. "How Do I Love Thee?" *Ensign*, Nov. 2003.
38. See, for example, Luke 7:11–15, the account of Jesus feeling compassion for a widow and raising her son from the dead.
39. This story comes from the personal experience of Don Staheli.
40. "Forget Me Not," *Ensign*, Nov. 2011.
41. See self-compassion.org
42. This story comes from the personal experience of Don Staheli.
43. This story comes from the personal experience of Don Staheli.
44. Robert Fulghum, *All I Really Need to Know I Learned in Kindergarten* (New York: Villard Books, 1990).
45. Marcus Tullius Cicero, Pro Plancio, 54 B.C.

ABOUT THE AUTHORS

DON H. STAHELI has served for over forty years in executive-level administrative positions for The Church of Jesus Christ of Latter-day Saints and as a Licensed Clinical Social Worker with LDS Family Services. He has fulfilled callings as president of the France Paris Mission, Regional Representative of the Twelve, stake president, bishop, and temple sealer, and he currently serves as a stake patriarch. He received a bachelor's degree in history and master's degrees in social work and international management. He is happily married to Cynthia Bodine Staheli. They have five children and twenty-one grandchildren.

LLOYD D. NEWELL holds an MA and a PhD from Brigham Young University, where he is a professor. The author or coauthor of more than a dozen books, he has addressed audiences in forty-six states and fifteen countries through his

ABOUT THE AUTHORS

seminars and other speaking engagements. He worked as a television news anchor in Utah, Pennsylvania, and for CNN in Atlanta, Georgia. Since 1990, he has served as announcer and writer for the nationwide weekly Mormon Tabernacle Choir broadcast *Music and the Spoken Word.* He and his wife, Karmel, are the parents of four children.